D0908804

Laura Ingalls Wilder

Doraine Bennett

rourkeeducationalmedia.com

Teacher Notes available at
rem4teachers.com

www.rourkeeducationalmedia.com

PHOTO CREDITS: Cover and title page: © AP Images; page 4: © Patricia Hofmeester; page 6: © Wikipedia; page 7: © red_frog; page 8: © Kyoungil Jeon; page 9a: © Scott Cartron; page 9b: © North Wind Pictures Archive; page 10, 11: © Laura Ingalls Wilder Memorial Society; page 13: © Library of Congress/Solomon D. Butcher; page 14, 15, 19: © Laura Ingalls Wilder Historic Home and Museum; page 17: © TimothyMN; page 21: © Wikipedia/Colin Faulkingham; page 22: © Wikipedia/NBC Television Network

Edited by: Precious McKenzie

Cover and interior design by: Renee Brady

Library of Congress PCN Data

Laura Ingalls Wilder / Bennett, Doraine (Little World Biographies)
ISBN 978-1-61810-160-0 (hard cover)(alk. paper)
ISBN 978-1-61810-293-5 (soft cover)
ISBN 978-1-61810-416-8 (e-Book)
Library of Congress Control Number: 2011945885

Rourke Educational Media
Printed in the United States of America,
North Mankato, Minnesota

rourkeeducationalmedia.com

customerservice@rourkeeducationalmedia.com • PO Box 643328 Vero Beach, Florida 32964

Table of Contents

Pioneers. 4

On the Move 6

Pioneer Life 8

Becoming Mary's Eyes 10

A Young Teacher. 12

Almanzo and Rose 14

Rocky Ridge Farm. 16

Remembering Pioneer Days . .18

Glossary 23

Index. 24

Pioneers

Can you imagine going on a journey in a covered wagon? Laura Ingalls Wilder and her family did. They were **pioneers**.

Fast Facts

A covered wagon was about half the length and half the width of a minivan. Families packed all their household goods, tools, and food inside.

On the Move

Replica of Laura's birth home.

Laura was born in a little log house. It sat near the Big Woods of Wisconsin. Laura said her father had "itchy feet" because he always wanted to move.

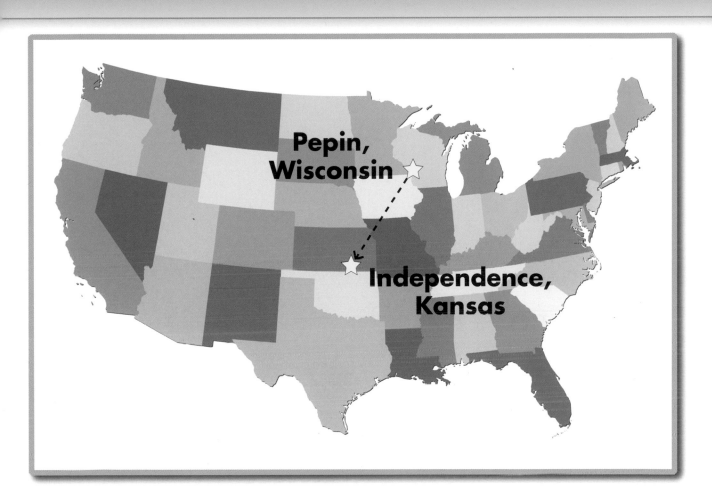

The United States government was giving away land to people who would move west and settle. The Ingalls family packed their covered wagon and headed to Kansas.

Pioneer Life

Pioneer life was not easy. Laura's mother made candles for light. Her father hunted and fished for meat. They grew their own vegetables, baked their own bread, and made their own clothes.

Laura and her family enjoyed their life. Laura's father played songs on his fiddle, and the girls sang and danced.

When Laura was seven, her family moved to Walnut Grove, Minnesota. They lived in a dugout home the first winter.

Becoming Mary's Eyes

Winters were very cold, and blizzards were dangerous. The family moved to town and lived in Pa's store each winter.

One winter, Laura's sister, Mary, was very sick. The sickness caused Mary to go blind.

Mary Ingalls

Pa told Laura she would have to be Mary's eyes. Laura described the land after a storm, people and their clothes, and the way light shone through the trees.

A Young Teacher

The Ingalls family moved to De Smet, Dakota Territory, in 1879. Laura liked going to school in De Smet. She was a good student. She wasn't quite sixteen years old when the school board asked her to become a teacher.

A one room schoolhouse was typical on the frontier. Students of different ages attended class together, with the same teacher.

13

Almanzo and Rose

Rose Wilder

A young farmer named Almanzo Wilder began coming to see Laura. Laura and Almanzo married the next year. Before long they had a baby girl named Rose.

Farm life was hard. The crops failed. Almanzo became very sick.

Rocky Ridge Farm

They packed up their covered wagon and moved on. They finally settled in Mansfield, Missouri, at Rocky Ridge Farm. Laura kept a **diary** of all the things that happened on their journey.

Laura's daughter grew up on Rocky Ridge Farm. Laura told Rose stories, just like Pa had told Laura stories when she was a child.

One day the owner of a newspaper asked Laura to write for him. She wrote poems, **essays**, and articles about farming.

Remembering Pioneer Days

Laura wanted to write stories about growing up in the pioneer days. She wanted people to remember what life was like.

Fast Facts

Laura was a teacher, a farmer, a public speaker, and a writer.

Historic societies have preserved Laura's home and belongings, like her desk where she wrote her famous stories.

Children loved Laura's book. They wrote letters to her asking for more stories. Her third book was *Little House on the Prairie*.

Children all over the world read Laura's books. The books were even published in **Braille** for blind children to read.

Surveyors' House.
De Smet, South Dakota.

People are fascinated by the way pioneers lived long ago.

Many people travel to the places Laura lived to see her little houses.

Laura died when she was 90 years old. The television show, Little House on the Prairie, was based on Laura's stories.

Melissa Gilbert as Laura Ingalls Wilder.

Timeline

1867 —	Laura born (February 7)
1869 —	Moved to Independence, Kansas
1874 —	Moved to Walnut Grove, Minnesota
1879 —	Moved to De Smet, Dakota Territory
1932 —	Little House in the Big Woods published
1933 —	Farmer Boy published
1935 —	Little House on the Prairie published
1957 —	Laura died

Glossary

Braille (brayl): a system of writing and printing for blind people, using raised dots felt with the fingertips

diary (dye-uh-ree): a book in which people write down things that happen each day, either to use as a record or to plan ahead

essays (ess-ayz): a piece of writing about a particular subject

pioneers (pye-uh-neerz): someone who explores unknown territory and settles there

Index

blind   10, 20
books   20
covered wagon   4, 16

pioneer(s)   4, 8, 18
teacher   12

Websites

www.liwfrontiergirl.com

www.lauraingallswilderhome.com/kids.htm

www.walnutgrove.org

About the Author

Doraine Bennett lives in Georgia with her husband. She loved reading the Little House books as a girl. She enjoys growing flowers, catching tadpoles in the creek behind her house, and writing books for children.

Ask The Author!
www.rem4students.com